W9-AFV-171

THOMAS JEFFERSON

Forerunner
to the Restoration

A Comparison of the Views of
Thomas Jefferson
and
Joseph Smith
on Government,
Education and Religion

THOMAS JEFFERSON

Forerunner
to the Restoration

A Comparison of the Views of
Thomas Jefferson
and
Joseph Smith
on Government,
Education and Religion

John J Stewart

Copyright © 1997 By
HORIZON PUBLISHERS & DISTRIBUTORS, INC.

All rights reserved.
Reproduction in whole or any parts thereof in any form
or by any media without written permission is prohibited.

First Printing: April 1997

International Standard Book Number:
0-88290-605-4

Horizon Publishers' Catalog and Order Number:
1961

Printed and distributed
in the United States of America by

**Horizon
Publishers**
& Distributors, Incorporated
P.O. Box 490 Bountiful, Utah 84011-0490

"The genuine and simple religion of Jesus will one day be restored; such as it was preached and practiced by Himself."

— Thomas Jefferson, in 1820,
the year of Joseph Smith's First Vision

Contents

*To
Robert*

I

Jefferson's Greatest Role: A Forerunner of the Restoration

T he epitaph Thomas Jefferson wished to have placed on his headstone was this:

> *Here was buried Thomas Jefferson, Author of the Declaration of American Independence, of the Statute of Virginia for Religious Freedom, and Father of the University of Virginia.*

In this statement can be seen the three qualities that Jefferson prized most in life: independence, religious freedom, and education—that is, the attainment of knowledge, wisdom and understanding.

Had he chosen to do so, he might also have included such items as these in his epitaph:

Member of the Continental Congress, Member of the Virginia Legislature, Governor of Virginia, United States Minister to France, U.S. Secretary of State, Vice President of the United States, one of the Framers of the Constitution's Bill of Rights, Founder of the Republican-Democratic Party, President of the American Philosophical Society.

MODEL FOR STATE CAPITOL. This plaster model, made in France under Jefferson's direction, is housed today in the State Capitol in Richmond, Virginia. It was inspired by a Roman ruin in Nimes, France which Jefferson said he gazed at for "whole hours . . . like a lover at his mistress."

And of course, he is best remembered as the third, and one of the three greatest, Presidents of the United States. Perhaps he was the greatest.

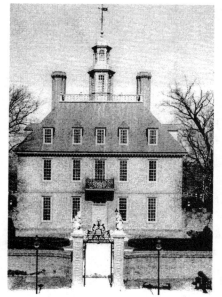

GOVERNORS' PALACE (RESTORED), WILLIAMSBURG
As a college student, Jefferson was in demand at Governor Fauquier's parties, first as a fiddler and then as a conversationalist. In 1779 he moved in as second Governor of the Commonwealth of Virginia.

Probably no other person in world history has such an outstanding record of public office and accomplishments in government as does Thomas Jefferson.

He was also a skilled architect, an inventor, an agriculturist, a writer and a musician. He is one of the most frequently quoted of all Americans, from such bits of sage advice as, "Never put off until tomorrow what you can do today," to the famous passages of the Declaration of Independence such as: ". . . Life, Liberty and the Pursuit of Happiness."

In April, 1962, at a White House dinner and reception honoring Nobel prize winners, President John F. Kennedy, the host, remarked, "I think this is the most extraordinary collection of talent, of human knowledge, that has ever been gathered together at the White House—with the possible exception of when Thomas Jefferson dined alone!"

No doubt many others would agree with that assessment of Jefferson. Numerous books have been written in praise of him.

Yet, the greatest role which Jefferson played has never been generally recognized as such, although in some future generation it most surely will be. This is his role as one who helped prepare the way for the great Latter-day Prophet Joseph Smith in the restoration of the true Gospel and Church of Jesus Christ; in the ushering in of the glorious, long-awaited Dispensation of the Fullness of Times, in preparation for the Second Coming of the Savior.

To people ignorant of the facts, this assertion of Thomas Jefferson's key role in life may seem surprising, especially when we remember that in his day he was accused by clergymen, journalists and political foes as being an atheist, an infidel and an adulterer. Such unfounded accusations against his name continue even in our day by character assassins writing spurious biographies.

II

America Divinely Established

One of the basic doctrines of The Church of Jesus Christ of Latter-day Saints (also known as LDS and Mormon) is the principle of fore-ordination. Not pre-destination, but fore-ordination. That is, the belief that some choice spirits in pre-mortal life were fore-ordained to fill certain missions or roles here upon the earth, provided they live worthily. Nevertheless, they have their free agency and may or may not perform the mission for which they were designated. Thus they are not pre-destined.

In a revelation given through the Prophet Joseph Smith in 1833, when the Saints were suffering horrible persecution in the slave state of Missouri and were refused protection by the state and federal authorities, the Lord Jesus Christ declared:

It is my will that they [the Latter-day Saints] should continue to importune for redress, and redemption, by the hands of those who are placed as rulers and are in authority over you, according to the laws and constitution of the people, which I have suffered to be established, and should be maintained for the rights and protection of all flesh, according to just and holy principles; that every man may act in doctrine and principle pertaining to futurity, according to the moral agency which I have given unto him, that every man may be accountable for his own sins in the day of judgment.

Therefore, it is not right that any man should be in bondage one to another.

And *for this purpose have I established the Constitution of this land, by the hands of wise men whom I raised up unto this very purpose*, and redeemed the land by the shedding of blood.[1]

In the Book of Mormon there are numerous prophecies concerning the founding of this nation. Referring primarily to its political form of government, it states that America is to be a land "choice above all other lands" on the face of the earth. The political liberty and prosperity foretold are dependent upon the people's righteousness. For instance, in recording the self-destruction of the Jaredites the Prophet Moroni, whose likeness appears atop several LDS temples today, comments:

> And now, we can behold the decrees of God concerning this land, that it is a land of promise; and whatsoever nation shall possess it shall serve God, or they shall be swept off when the fullness of his wrath shall come upon them. And the fullness of his wrath cometh upon them when they are ripened in iniquity.[2]

This warning, coupled with a great promise, seems to have been included specifically for our benefit today:

> And this cometh unto you, O ye Gentiles, that ye may repent, and not continue in your iniquities until the fullness come, that ye may not bring down the fullness of the wrath of God upon you as the inhabitants of the land have hitherto done. Behold, this is a choice land, and whatsoever nation shall possess it shall be free from bondage, and from captivity, and from all other nations under heaven, if they will but serve the God of the land, who is Jesus Christ, who hath been manifested by the things which we have written.[3]

---

1. *Doctrine and Covenants* 101:76-80.
2. Ether 2:9.
3. Ether 2:11-12.

So, from both the book of Doctrine and Covenants and the Book of Mormon we learn of the Divine direction in events leading to the formation of this nation.

George Washington, John Adams, Samuel Adams, Benjamin Franklin, Thomas Paine, James Madison, Nathan Hale, Patrick Henry, Richard Henry Lee, and our other founding fathers were "wise men raised up unto this very purpose." They were fore-ordained. And the foremost intellect among them, the man they chose to write the Declaration of Independence, was Thomas Jefferson.

In his biography of the Prophet Joseph Smith, the late Dr. John A. Widtsoe, a member of the LDS Council of Twelve Apostles and a former president of two universities, reminds us of the role the Prophet's family played in the founding of our nation:

> During the Revolutionary period and before, many of Joseph Smith's ancestors, on both paternal and maternal sides, took courageous and unflinching part in the movements, including army service, that led to the formation of the United States. Joseph Smith's great-grandfather, Samuel Smith, took part officially in several activities that led to the break between America and the mother country. He was chairman of the 'tea committee' in 1773, when disputes arose with England over taxation. Though of advanced age, he served honorably in the army of the Revolution. His son, Asael, Joseph Smith's grandfather, . . . also served honorably in the army of the Revolution.[4]

At LDS General Conferences on September 16, 1877, and again on April 10, 1898, Wilford Woodruff, fourth President of the LDS Church, declared:

> Those men who laid the foundation of this American government and signed the Declaration of Independence were

---

4. *Joseph Smith, Seeker After Truth, Prophet of God*, p. 100.

the best spirits the God of Heaven could find on the face of the earth. They were choice spirits . . . inspired of the Lord.

Every one of those men that signed the Declaration of Independence . . . called upon me, as an Apostle of the Lord Jesus Christ, in the Temple at St. George two consecutive nights and demanded at my hands that I should go forth and attend to the ordinances of the house of God for them. . . .

Would those spirits have called upon me, as an Elder in Israel, to perform that work if they had not been noble spirits before God? They would not. . . . Said they: . . . 'We laid the foundation of the government you now enjoy, and we never apostatized from it, but we remained true to it and were faithful to God.'[5]

Obviously all these wise men, these founding fathers, and their supportive wives, played important roles in helping prepare for the Restoration of the Gospel and Church. To emphasize Jefferson's particular role is in no wise meant to belittle that of his contemporaries, those choice men whom God "raised up unto this very purpose" who also appeared to President Wilford Woodruff in the Saint George Temple, requesting that earthly ordinances be performed for them.

Jefferson's extensive writings provide a helpful insight to the unfortunate conditions in society with which the young Prophet Joseph had to contend, in New York, New England, and in the slave state of Missouri and elsewhere, as he attempted to fulfill his mission of restoration.

---

5. *Journal of Discourses*, Vol. 19, p. 229, and *Report of General Conference*, April 10, 1898, pp. 89-90; also, *The Vision*, by N. B. Lundwall, pp. 98-101.

III

A Look at Jefferson's Brilliant Life

B efore reviewing these specific issues, let's review a brief biographical sketch of this genius of Monticello, to whom all Americans and citizens of many other countries are indebted for his powerful influence in advancing the cause of individual liberty and freedoms.

Based again on the reality of fore-ordination, Jefferson was born at the right time, in the right family and in the right place to fulfill his important mission in life. Of all the thirteen colonies, Virginia was the most politically influential, with a citizenry that included George Washington, Patrick Henry, George Wythe, George Mason, Peyton Randolph, Richard Henry Lee, James Madison, James Monroe, and dozens of other men of prominence who would be an influence for good in his life.

He was especially fortunate in his parentage: his father, Peter Jefferson, of Welch ancestry, was a large and physically powerful man with a keen intellect and seemingly endless energy and ambition. He was a successful farmer, surveyor, map maker, sheriff and county political leader. Peter's grandfather, Thomas Jefferson, and his father, Thomas II, were both prominent, successful men. Peter owned several thousand acres of land and dozens of Negro slaves. He instilled in his son an interest in politics and a desire to attain a formal education, as well as a love of the soil and an appreciation of the beauties of nature. Peter's wife was Jane Randolph. The Randolphs were one of the wealthiest and most prestigious families in Virginia, dating back to her grandfather, William Randolph, (1651-1711), Virginia's Attorney-General.

Thomas was Jefferson's third of ten children. As the oldest son he inherited most of the estate, although his sisters and his brother also received a substantial inheritance. Tom was born on April 13, 1743, at the Jeffersons' Shadwell plantation near Charlottesville. Two years later, William Randolph, Mrs. Jefferson's cousin and a close friend of her husband, died. Anticipating his death, William asked the Jeffersons to move to his estate in Tuckahoe on the James River a few miles above Richmond. Here Tom spent the next seven years, living with the combined Jefferson and Randolph families. When his family moved back to Shadwell, Tom spent a portion of his time in a boarding school where he learned Latin, French, and Greek from the Reverend William Douglas.

Tom had a deep love and respect for his father, and one of the most traumatic days of his life came at the age of fourteen when his father died. Shortly after that he entered another school a few miles from Shadwell to study under the Reverend James Maury, a much better instructor than Douglas. But perhaps the greatest influence on his life at the time was his older sister Jane, who encouraged him in education and in learning the violin and other fine arts. Her sudden death when Tom was twenty-two caused him another deep sorrow.

At seventeen, with a desire to broaden his education, he traveled by horse the hundred miles to Williamsburg, then the capital of Virginia, where he enrolled in the College of William and Mary, with its seven-man faculty, to study law, mathematics, philosophy, music, and the classics. By now he was a lanky six-foot-two, with red hair, freckles, and a high-pitched voice.

At Williamsburg he fortunately came under the influence of William Small, an inspiring Scots professor of mathematics

George Wythe

and philosophy, and George Wythe, a prominent lawyer and professor of law, with whom he studied. His friendship with them and his family relationship to the Randolphs gave him entry to the highest social and political circles, as well as motivation to study hard and make a success of his life. The three of them, Small, Wythe, and young Tom, would occasionally dine together in the Colonial Governor's Palace with the acting Royal Governor, Francis Fauquier.

In an autobiographical sketch Jefferson described the great influence Small had upon him:

> It was my great good fortune, and what probably fixed the destinies of my life, that Dr. William Small of Scotland was then professor of mathematics, a man profound in most of the useful branches of science, with a happy and an enlarged and liberal mind. He, most happily for me, became soon attached to me and made me his daily companion when not engaged in the school, and from his conversation I got my first views of the expansion of science and of the system of things in which we are placed. Fortunately the philosophical chair became vacant soon after my arrival at college and he was appointed to fill it . . .

It was Professor Small who introduced Tom to three famous Englishmen whose writings had a profound influence on his life and especially on his political views:

Francis Bacon (1561-1626), a philosopher and statesman who became Lord Chancellor to King James I, but is chiefly remembered for the stimulus he gave to scientific research in England,

John Locke (1632-1704), an empiricist philosopher whose writings helped initiate the period of European Enlightenment, and

Sir Isaac Newton (1642-1726), regarded by many as the most prestigious natural philosopher and mathematician of modern times; president of the Royal Society of London.

WREN BUILDING, COLLEGE OF WILLIAM AND MARY
Here, in America's second oldest college, seventeen year-old Thomas Jefferson was introduced to the philosophy of the Enlightenment.

So enthralled was young Jefferson with the writings of these intellectual giants and the lectures and private conversations of Professor Small, that he largely refrained from the social and entertainment enticements of Williamsburg and concentrated on his studies, laboring at times fifteen hours per day.

Marries Beautiful Widow

But he also found time for romance. After a number of flirtations with various women, he married a beautiful twenty-three-year-old widow, Martha "Patty" Wayles Skelton, on New Year's Day, 1772, at Forest Plantation, home of her wealthy thrice widowed father, Attorney John Wayles. The marriage doubled his land holdings. Tom was twenty-eight. Martha shared his love of music and other fine arts as well as horse riding and the great out-of-doors. She played the piano and harpsichord, he played the violin and they played and also sang duets. It was a great match.

Martha had a son by her first marriage and Jefferson happily anticipated adopting him, but the boy died seven months before their marriage, at the age of four.

With his inherited wealth and his income as a lawyer, Jefferson built his famous mansion which is still known today as Monticello (Italian for "little mountain.") It was largely of his

MONTICELLO, near Charlottesville, Virginia.
The name in Italian means "Little Mountain."
It's located on a 500-foot high hill.

own architectural design, and stands on a five-hundred-foot-high hill near Charlottesville, Virginia, affording a magnificent view of the surrounding countryside. He sent to Europe for the finest available piano to place in it for his happy bride.

Although theirs was a congenial marriage, built on devotion to each other, it was also racked with sorrow: of their six children, five daughters and one son, four died in infancy. Only their first child, Martha "Patsy," and their fourth child, Mary "Polly Maria," grew to maturity. They both married. Only Martha survived her father.

Mrs. Jefferson, long in fragile health, died September 6, 1782, four months after the birth of their sixth child and less than eleven years after their marriage. Upon her death bed she requested that Jefferson never remarry, and he never did.

Tom's sister Martha married his closest friend, Dabney Carr. Tom and Dabney had been companions in youth and served together in the Virginia House of Burgesses. Prior to Martha Jefferson's death, Dabney died suddenly, whereupon Tom took his sister Martha and her children into his own home.

Martha Jefferson Randolph

With the death of his wife and four children and other loved ones, Jefferson developed a disdain for the medical profession. Whenever he saw two doctors conferring he looked for a buzzard—the sign of death. His own formula for good health was to soak his feet in cold water each evening, whether summer or winter, eat an abundance of vegetables and very little meat, and get plenty of exercise.

Jefferson was a man of so many talents and interests, and assumed so many responsibilities, both private and public, it's a wonder that he ever found any time for sleep.

Although he wrote only one book, he wrote numerous official documents in the various public offices he held, and he was a prolific correspondent, writing some twenty-five thousand letters to individuals. Fortunately for posterity he kept a copy of many of these, thus affording later generations an unusually good insight to his character and interests.

In April, 1794, he wrote to John Adams from Monticello:

> I return to farming with ardor which I scarcely knew in my youth, and which has got the better entirely of my love of study. Instead of writing 10 or 12 letters a day, which I have been in the habit of doing as a thing of course, I put off answering my letters now, farmerlike, till a rainy day and then find it sometimes postponed by other necessary occupations.

John Adams

Are his letters prized today? On October 30, 1986, appeared a lengthy newspaper article under the headline, "Jefferson letter brings world record." The first paragraph states: "New York (UPI)— A one-page letter by Thomas Jefferson decrying anti-Semitism and 'the universal spirit of religious intolerance' was sold for $396,000—the most ever paid at auction for a letter or presidential document. . . ."

From early manhood Jefferson felt constantly torn between political duty to country and his desire for the private life of a country gentleman on his vast estate at Monticello. It was a long established Southern tradition that men of wealth had a responsibility to serve society in offices of public trust. Jefferson could not ignore this. Nor could he ignore the growing discontent with the behavior of the mother country, England, toward the American Colonies, and the resulting cry for independence.

Begins His Political Career

Two years after being admitted to the Virginia bar to practice law in 1767, he entered actively into politics in 1769 as a member of the Virginia House of Burgesses. He soon became an influential member of that legislative body.

In its stupidity the British Parliament, in 1774, passed five acts, known to history as the Intolerable Acts or Coercive Acts, largely in retaliation for the Boston Tea Party—the colonists' protest against taxation without representation. These five acts penalized the colonists in various ways, suspending many of the rights they had previously enjoyed. These drastic measures were protested throughout all thirteen colonies and resulted in the calling of the First Continental Congress and subsequently the Revolutionary War.

Jefferson's response to the Intolerable Acts was to write a persuasive essay entitled "A Summary View of the Rights of British America," in which he declared that Britain had no right of government in the American Colonies. This, of course, was considered a treasonous document. As author of it Jefferson was eligible to be hanged in London. That was a risk he was willing to take. One of the many points of grievance he expressed against England was that it had forced the practice of slavery and the slave trade upon the American colonists.

Jefferson concluded his essay with some free advice to his majesty George III:

> These are our grievances which we have thus laid before his majesty with that freedom of language and sentiment which becomes a free people, claiming their rights as derived from the laws of nature, and not as the gift of their chief magistrate. Let those flatter, who fear; it is not an American art. To give praise where it is not due, might be well from the venal, but would ill beseem those who are asserting the rights of human nature. They know, and will therefore say, that kings are the servants, not the proprietors, of the people.
>
> Open your breast, Sire, to liberal and expanded thought. Let not the name of George the third be a blot in the page of history. . . .

Whether or not King George read the essay, thousands of Americans and British did, as it was soon printed and reprinted in pamphlet form throughout the Colonies and in England. Many thought it was too strong a statement, while others delighted in it. As a result of its publication, Jefferson's name became a household word on both sides of the Atlantic. It helped place him in a position of leadership among the American revolutionists.

At a special meeting of the House of Burgesses in March 1775, known as the Virginia Convention, Jefferson was elected

Peyton Randolph

to a committee of twelve to plan for a Virginia Militia in face of the possibility of war with England. He was also elected as an alternate delegate to the Second Continental Congress in Philadelphia. Virginia's seven delegates to the First Continental Congress were all reelected: Peyton Randolph, George Washington, Patrick Henry, Richard Henry Lee, Benjamin Harrison, Richard Bland, and Edmund Pendleton. But due to other obligations at Williamsburg Peyton Randolph was unable to attend the Second Congress, so Jefferson was able to go in his stead.

Here he became acquainted with Benjamin Franklin, John and Samuel Adams, John Hancock and other leading statesmen from the various colonies. It was at this Congress that John Adams nominated Washington to be commander of the Continental Army, a position to which John Hancock aspired, and which Washington claimed he did not desire. He told Patrick Henry he feared that he would fail and his reputation would be ruined. But the fact that he had worn a military uniform to each session of the Congress seemed to indicate a desire for the job.

As the likelihood of war increased Jefferson, like many others, still expressed the hope that it could be averted and that the thirteen colonies could continue their affiliation with England, if only King George and the British Parliament would mend their ways and respect the rights of the Americans.

To Jefferson's sorrow, his cousin and friend, John Randolph, brother of Peyton, chose to move to England rather than break with the mother country. Likewise did Benjamin Franklin's son and hundreds of others.

But by the spring of 1776 a preponderance of the colonists favored separation from England, even if it meant war to achieve it. On instructions from the Virginia Convention to its delegates in Congress, on June 7, Richard Henry Lee proposed: "Resolved, that these United Colonies are, and of right ought to be, free and independent States; and that they are absolved from all allegiance to the British Crown, and that all political connection between them and the State of Great Britain is, and ought to be, totally dissolved."

For four days the Congress considered this resolution along with related items. On June 11, it was decided to appoint a committee of five to prepare a Declaration in support of the Resolution. As the presenter of the Resolution Mr. Lee would have been a likely choice to head the committee, but he had suddenly been called back to Virginia because of his wife's serious illness. So another Virginian, thirty-three-year-old Thomas Jefferson, was selected, he having achieved the reputation of a skillful writer and one who fully shared Lee's sentiments. The other four committeemen named were Benjamin Franklin, seventy, from Pennsylvania; John Adams, forty, from Massachusetts; Roger Sherman, fifty-five, from Connecticut, and Robert R. Livingston, twenty-nine, from New York.

Writes Declaration of Independence

In deference to John Adams, a delegate from Massachusetts where fighting had already occurred, Jefferson as chairman invited him to draft the Declaration. But Adams declined, insisting that it would be better for Jefferson as a Virginian to do so, Virginia being the dominant colony. Actually Jefferson was delighted with the opportunity.

In the Declaration he repeated the same sentiments that he had earlier expressed in his "Summary View of the Rights of British America" and in other documents he had recently drafted, including his version of a new constitution of Virginia. He also incorporated ideas that had been expressed by James Wilson, Richard Henry Lee, George Mason, John Locke and others. Members of his committee suggested minor changes before it was presented to the entire Congress, on June 28.

For several days the delegates read and debated the draft as it came from the committee. Before it was finally approved one-fourth of it had been deleted and other parts amended. Jefferson anguished over the deletions and changes that were inflicted on his manuscript. He was especially disappointed that his denunciation of slavery and the slave trade had again been deleted, just as it had been in his "Summary" document. Not only South Carolina and Georgia delegates were opposed, but some of New England's as well, for powerful men there had achieved their wealth through the slave trade.

Throughout the remainder of his life Jefferson felt that his prize document had been sadly weakened by the congressional editing to which it was subjected by the fifty-five delegates. He sent copies of his original version and the final adopted version to Richard Henry Lee and several other friends so that they could pass judgment on the comparative merits of the two. Those who have since studied the two versions are of varying opinions in regard to their literary and political merits.

During the days of debate on it Benjamin Franklin sat by Jefferson's side, offering him words of consolation and telling him that he, Ben, had long ago decided to never write another document for submission to a public body. Jefferson was especially appreciative of the total support John Adams gave to it during the debate.

On the hot and muggy day of July 4, 1776, the Declaration of Independence in its amended form was passed. Then it was that Benjamin Franklin admonished his

Benjamin Franklin

fellow congressmen that they must now all hang together or they would all surely hang separately.

The Declaration of Independence

These powerful words written by Thomas Jefferson radically shaped the course of this nation and of the world:

> When in the Course of human events, it becomes necessary for one people to dissolve the political bands which have connected them with another, and to assume among the powers of the earth, the separate and equal station to which the Laws of Nature and of Nature's God entitle them, a decent respect to the opinions of mankind requires that they should declare the causes which impel them to the separation.
>
> We hold these truths to be self-evident, that all men are created equal, that they are endowed by their Creator with certain unalienable Rights, that among these are Life, Liberty and the pursuit of Happiness.
>
> That to secure these rights, Governments are instituted among Men, deriving their just powers from the consent of the governed. That whenever any Form of Government becomes destructive of these ends, it is the Right of the People to alter or to abolish it, and to institute new Government, laying its foundation on such principles and organizing its powers in such form, as to them shall seem most likely to effect their Safety and Happiness.
>
> Prudence, indeed, will dictate that Governments long established should not be changed for light and transient causes; and accordingly all experience hath shewn, that mankind are more disposed to suffer, while evils are sufferable, than to right themselves by abolishing the forms to which they are accustomed. But when a long train of abuses and usurpations, pursuing invariably the same Object evinces a design to reduce them under absolute Despotism, it is their right, it is their duty, to throw off such Government, and to provide new Guards for their future security.

Such has been the patient sufferance of these Colonies; and such is now the necessity which constrains them to alter their former Systems of Government. The history of the present King of Great Britain is a history of repeated injuries and usurpations, all having in direct object the establishment of an absolute Tyranny over these States. . . .

We, therefore, the Representatives of the United States of America, in General Congress, Assembled, appealing to the Supreme Judge of the world for the rectitude of our intentions, do, in the Name, and by the Authority of the good People of these Colonies, solemnly publish and declare, That these United Colonies are, and of Right ought to be *Free and Independent States*; that they are Absolved from all Allegiance to the British Crown, and that all political connection between them and the State of Great Britain, is and ought to be totally dissolved; and that as Free and Independent States, they have full Power to levy War, conclude Peace, contract Alliances, establish Commerce, and to do all other Acts and Things which Independent States may of right do.

And for the support of this Declaration, with a firm reliance on the protection of divine Providence, we mutually pledge to each other our Lives, our Fortunes and our sacred Honor.

Recalls How Declaration Was Passed

In Jefferson's autobiography, written many years later, he recounted the deliberations that led to the preparation and passage of the Declaration:

On the 15th of May, 1776, the convention of Virginia instructed their delegates in Congress to propose to that body to declare the colonies independent of G. Britain, and appointed a commee [committee] to prepare a declaration of rights and plan of government.

In Congress, Friday June 7. 1776. The delegates from Virginia moved in obedience to instructions from their constituents that the Congress should declare that these United colonies are & of right ought to be free & independent states, that they are absolved from all allegiance to the British crown, and that all political connection between them & the state of Great Britain is & ought to be, totally dissolved; that measures should be immediately taken for procuring the assistance of foreign powers, and a Confederation be formed to bind the colonies more closely together.

The house being obliged to attend at that time to some other business, the proposition was referred to the next day, when the members were ordered to attend punctually at ten o'clock.

Saturday June 8. They proceeded to take it into consideration and referred it to a committee of the whole, into which they immediately resolved themselves, and passed that day & Monday the 10th in debating on the subject.

It was argued by Wilson, Robert R. Livingston, E. Rutledge, Dickinson and others.

That tho' they were friends to the measures themselves, and saw the impossibility that we should ever again be united with Gr. Britain, yet they were against adopting them at this time:

That the conduct we had formerly observed was wise & proper now, of deferring to take any capital step till the voice of the people drove us into it:

That the people of the middle colonies (Maryland, Delaware, Pennsylva, the Jerseys & N. York) were not yet ripe for bidding adieu to British connection, but that they were fast ripening & in short time would join in the general voice of America. . . .

That it would not be long before we should receive certain information of the disposition of the French court, from the agent whom we had sent to Paris for that purpose:

That if this disposition should be favorable, by waiting the event of the present campaign, which we all hoped would be successful, we should have reason to expect an alliance on better terms:

That this would in fact work no delay of any effectual aid from such ally, as, from the advance of the season & distance of our situation, it was impossible we could receive any assistance during this campaign:

That it was prudent to fix among ourselves the terms on which we should form alliance, before we declared we would form one at all events:

And that if these were agreed on, & our Declaration of Independence ready by the time our Ambassador should be prepared to sail, it would be as well as to go into that Declaration at this day.

On the other side it was urged by J. Adams, Lee, Wythe, and others

That no gentleman had argued against the policy or the right of separation from Britain, nor had supposed it possible we should ever renew our connection; that they had only opposed its being now declared:

That as to the people or parliament of England, we had alwais been independent of them, their restraints on our trade deriving efficacy from our acquiescence only, & not from any rights they possessed of imposing them, & that so far our connection had been federal only & was now dissolved by the commencement of hostilities:

That as to the King, we had been bound to him by allegiance, but that this bond was now dissolved by his assent to the late act of parliament, by which he declares us out of his protection, and by his levying war on us, a fact which had long ago proved us out of his protection; it being a certain position in law that allegiance & protection are reciprocal, the one ceasing when the other is withdrawn. . .

And that the only misfortune is that we did not enter into alliance with France six months sooner, as besides opening their ports for the vent of our last year's produce, they might have marched an army into Germany and prevented the petty princes there from selling their unhappy subjects to subdue us.

It appearing in the course of these debates that the colonies of N. York, New Jersey, Pennsylvania, Delaware, Maryland, and South Carolina were not yet matured for falling from the parent stem, but that they were fast advancing to that state, it was thought most prudent to wait a while for them, and to postpone the final decision to July 1. but that this might occasion as little delay as possible a committee was appointed to prepare a declaration of independence. The commee were J. Adams, Dr. Franklin, Roger Sherman, Robert Livingston & myself. Committees were also appointed at the same time to prepare a plan of confederation for the colonies, and to state the terms proper to be proposed for foreign alliance. The committee for drawing the declaration of Independence desired me to do it. It was accordingly done, and being approved by them, I reported it to the house on Friday the 28th of June when it was read and ordered to lie on the table. On Monday, the 1st of July the house resolved itself into a commee of the whole & resumed the consideration of the original motion made by the delegates of Virginia, which being again debated through the day, was carried in the affirmative by the votes of N. Hamshire, Connecticut, Massachusetts, Rhode Island, N. Jersey, Maryland, Virginia, N. Carolina, & Georgia. S. Carolina and Pennsylvania voted against it. Delaware having but two members present, they were divided. The delegates for New York declared they were for it themselves & were assured their constituents were for it, but that their instructions having been drawn near a twelvemonth before, when reconciliation was still the general object, they were enjoined by them to do nothing which should impede that object. They therefore thought themselves not justifiable in voting on either side, and asked leave to withdraw from the question, which was given them. The commee rose & reported their resolution to the house. Mr. Edward Rutledge of S. Carolina then requested the determination might be put off to the next day, as he believed his colleagues, tho' they disapproved of the resolution, would then join in it for the sake of unanimity. The ultimate question whether the house would agree to the resolution of the committee was accordingly postponed to the next day, when it was again moved and S. Carolina concurred in voting for it. In the meantime a third member had come post from Delaware counties and turned the vote of that colony in favour of the resolution. Members of a different sentiment attended that morning from Pennsylvania also, their vote was changed, so that the whole 12 colonies who were authorized to vote at all, gave their voices for it; and within a few days, the convention of N. York approved of it and thus supplied the void occasioned by the withdrawing of her delegates from the vote.

Congress proceeded the same day to consider the declaration of Independence which had been reported & lain on the table the Friday preceding, and on Monday referred to a commee of the whole. The pusillanimous idea that we had friends in England worth keeping terms with, still haunted the minds of many. For this reason those passages which conveyed censures on the people of England were struck out, lest they should give them offence. The clause too, reprobating the enslaving the inhabitants of Africa, was struck out in complaisance to South Carolina and Georgia, who had never attempted to restrain the importation of slaves, and who on the contrary still wished to continue it. Our northern brethren also I believe felt a little tender under those censures; for tho' their people have very few slaves themselves yet they had been pretty considerable carriers of them to others. The debates having taken up the greater parts of the 2d 3d & 4th days of July were, in the evening of the last, closed the declaration was reported by the commee, agreed to by the house and signed by every member present except Mr. Dickinson.

Prepares Historic Bills in Virginia

After passage of the Declaration of Independence Jefferson continued in Congress at Philadelphia another two months, until September 2, at which time he resigned and returned home, having been elected to the Virginia Legislature to represent his county. He spent a month with his family at Monticello, then traveled to Williamsburg for the opening of the Legislative Assembly on October 7.

> I knew that our legislation under the regal [British] government had many very vicious points which urgently required reformation, and I thought that I could be of more use in forwarding that work. I therefore retired from my seat in Congress.

During the first week Jefferson introduced three significant bills designed to upgrade the quality of life in Virginia, and hopefully by example in the other colonies (or states) as well. Within that first week he achieved passage of two of the bills, one to establish courts of justice and the other to abolish the aristocratic land laws, known as entail and primogeniture, thus making it possible for owners to divide up their lands as they saw fit for purposes of inheritance or resale. Within a few days he also achieved passage of a bill for a general revision and codification of the fundamental laws of Virginia, and was named chairman of a committee to execute this work.

He failed to achieve passage of a "Bill for the More General Diffusion of Knowledge." He strongly believed that freedom could not survive in ignorance and thus he sought to establish a system for free and universal public education, for all children, rich and poor alike, in the elementary grades, the expenses to be borne by the citizens of each county. Jefferson said it failed to win approval because it placed on the wealthy the burden of providing education for the poor, and the legislators, being generally of the wealthy class, were unwilling to incur that burden. The failed bill also provided for the establishment of colleges "for a middle degree of instruction, calculated for the common purposes of life," and "an ultimate grade for teaching the sciences generally, & in their highest degree."

In his autobiography this wealthy son of aristocracy commented:

I considered 4 of these bills, passed or reported, as forming a system by which every fibre would be eradicated of antient [ancient] or future aristocracy; and a foundation laid for a government truly republican. The repeal of the laws of entail would prevent the accumulation and perpetuation of wealth in select families, and preserve the soil of the country from being absorbed in Mortmain. The abolition of primogeniture, and equal partition of inheritances removed the feudal and unnatural distinctions which made one member of every family rich, and all the rest poor, substituting equal partition, the best of all Agrarian laws. The restoration of the rights of conscience relieved the people from taxation for the support of a religion not theirs; for the establishment was truly of the religion of the rich, the dissenting sects being entirely composed of the less wealthy people; and these, by the bill for a general education, would be qualified to understand their rights, to maintain them, and to exercise with intelligence their parts in self-government: and all this would be effected without the violation of a single natural right of any one individual citizen.

Elected Governor of Virginia

Despite the fact that Jefferson had made enemies in the Virginia Legislature due to some of the bills he had introduced, he was elected Governor by the Assembly on June 1, 1779, succeeding Patrick Henry, who three years earlier had dramatically shouted, "Give me liberty or give me death!" Jefferson, now thirty-six years old, had lost some of his earlier esteem for Henry, concluding the fiery orator more windbag than statesman. He said he nearly prayed once that Henry would get the second alternative gift.

Patrick Henry

With the country in the midst of war against Great Britain, Jefferson found Virginia's affairs of state in a shambles. Wartime inflation had hit both the private and public sectors. The Assembly resorted to issuing paper money, which proved a poor expediency. British warships patrolling offshore reduced commerce to a trickle. Citizens refused to pay taxes, mostly because they had no funds with which to pay. The 1779 wheat crop was largely a failure, yielding hardly enough for seed for the ensuing year. Virginia had shared with North Carolina what little supply of armaments it had with which to equip a militia. Having sent many able-bodied Virginians off to the Continental armies, there was not a lot of manpower left in the state to resist an invasion.

Benedict Arnold, the former American general turned traitor, was now in command of a British force which sailed out of New York in early January 1781. He and his forces entered the James River and launched an attack on Richmond, burning the Foundry and destroying other buildings and supplies of munitions. Jefferson's anger toward Benedict Arnold was such that he offered a reward of five thousand guineas for his capture. Unfortunately he had no takers.

In May Arnold and also Major General William Phillips again led troops in attacks on Virginia towns, including Williamsburg and Richmond. Lord Charles Cornwallis invaded Virginia from the south and word was received that General Henry Clinton with his British forces was approaching from the north. The Virginia Assembly moved to Charlottesville for greater safety. Jefferson sent a desperate plea to General Washington to come to the rescue of his home state.

Jefferson's second one-year term of office expired on June 1, 1781. He was eligible for reelection but declined a third term, leaving it to the Assembly to choose a successor.

Shortly after the Assembly had moved to Charlottesville and Jefferson to his nearby home at Monticello the British sent a cavalry unit under the command of Lieutenant Colonel

Banastre Tarleton to Charlottesville and Monticello to capture Jefferson and other officials. Jefferson tells that a Mr. Jouett rushed ahead, riding all night, to warn them of the approaching cavalry, giving them time to escape both from Monticello and Charlottesville. Jefferson was appreciative of the fact that Tarleton gave his soldiers strict orders to disturb nothing at Monticello.

In contrast to Tarleton's courteous behavior, Lord Cornwallis encamped his army on Elkhill, another of Jefferson's estates, on the James River, where he wantonly destroyed the crops, burned the barns, stole or destroyed all the livestock, and carried off the thirty slaves, most of them later dying of small-pox to which they were exposed in the army camp. Jefferson estimated that Cornwallis captured thirty thousand slaves in Virginia. Twenty-seven thousand of them died of smallpox and camp fever, and the other three thousand were sent some to the West Indies and exchanged for rum, sugar, coffee and fruits, and some to New York, from whence they were eventually sent to Africa.

Writes a Book on Virginia

In the period between his retirement as governor and his appointment once again to Congress, Jefferson wrote a book, *Notes on the State of Virginia*, in response to a request he had received from an emissary of the French government. To pre-pare his manuscript with a minimum of interruptions Jefferson spent several weeks at Poplar Forest, a plantation he owned some ninety miles southwest of Monticello, near today's Lynchburg. Although a superb horseman, Jefferson fell from his horse one day, breaking an arm, which took six weeks to mend. This slowed his writing efforts, but it did not keep him from completing the project.

His book deals with every aspect of life in Virginia: the people, their customs, politics, the economy, the history, the geography, topography, the plants, the animals, the birds, any-thing and everything a stranger might wish to know. Its pages reflect Jefferson's pride in Virginia, his love of its mountains, valleys and rivers, and the thrill he felt in the wonders of nature.

Jefferson was busily engaged as a congressman from December, 1773 through May, 1774. He had taken his eleven-year-old daughter Martha "Patsy" with him to Philadelphia, only to find that the sessions of Congress had been shifted to Princeton, New Jersey, then to Annapolis, Maryland, due to interference from soldiers demanding higher pay. He left Martha with a friend in Philadelphia. Be it remembered that her mother had died the previous year. From Annapolis he wrote to Patsy:

> The conviction that you would be more improved in the situation I have placed you than if still with me, has solaced me on my parting with you, which my love for you has rendered a difficult thing. The acquirements which I hope you will make under the tutors I have provided for you will render you more worthy of my love, and if they cannot increase it they will prevent it's diminution. Consider the good lady who has taken you under her roof . . . as your mother, as the only person to whom, since the loss with which heaven has been pleased to afflict you, you can now look up. . . . With respect to the distribution of your time the following is what I should approve.
>
> from 8. to 10 o'clock practice music.
>
> from 10. to 1. dance one day and draw another.
>
> from 1. to 2. draw on the day you dance, and write a letter the next day.
>
> from 3. to 4. read French.
>
> from 4. to 5. exercise yourself in music.
>
> from 5. till bedtime read English, write &c. . . .

One can easily picture little Martha begging her father to take her with him, or take her back to family members in Monticello, rather than leaving her with strangers in Philadelphia. It must have been a terribly lonely time for her. Perhaps Jefferson felt the experience would help her mature. He was anxious for her to be well read so that when she had a family of her own she could give proper direction to her children. In view of the caliber of young men available he feared the chances were great that in marriage she would "draw a blockhead," and thus would have no assistance in guiding her children.

In another letter to Patsy, Jefferson urges her to always dress properly and cleanly from the moment she arises until going to bed. And in a third letter he seeks to calm her fears: she had heard that a recent earthquake meant that the world was coming to an end. Jefferson told her:

> I hope you will have good sense enough to disregard those foolish predictions that the world is to be at an end soon. The Almighty has never made known to any body at what time he created it, nor will he tell any body when he means to put an end to it, if ever he means to do it. As to preparations for that event, the best way is for you to be always prepared for it. The only way to be so is never to do nor say a bad thing. If ever you are about to say any thing amiss or to do any thing wrong, consider before hand. You will feel something within you which will tell you it is wrong and ought not to be said or done: this is your conscience, and be sure to obey it. Our maker has given us all, this faithful internal Monitor, and if you always obey it, you will always be prepared for the end of the world: or for a much more certain event which is death.

The brutal but bungling Cornwallis surrendered to Washington at Yorktown, Virginia, on October 19, 1781, but the war dragged on sporadically for nearly another two years, until the Treaty of Paris was signed in September, 1783, with the condition that it had to be ratified within six months by at least nine of the thirteen American states before it was official.

Jefferson was appointed chairman of the congressional committee to get the treaty ratified and back to Paris. By late December, with but two months remaining to the deadline, only seven of the states had delegates in Congress. Jefferson sent urgent letters to the others. Finally, three weeks later, delegates arrived from New Hampshire and New Jersey and the ratification papers prepared by Jefferson, assuring America's independence, were duly signed and sent, marking the official end of the Revolutionary War.

In that 1783-84 session of Congress Jefferson served as chairman of several key committees devoted to establishing a workable system of government for the new Republic. For example, he devised our coinage system, and later had the U. S. Mint established. He also took the lead in establishing a policy for settlement of the western territories beyond the frontier.

Virginia ceded to the national government the vast area it owned northwest of the Ohio River. In what came to be known as the Northwest Ordinance of 1784, Jefferson insisted that this land should not be considered colonial territory by any of the original thirteen states, but that it should be divided into areas that could eventually join the Union as states, with the same rights and standing as the original thirteen. This became the accepted pattern for all western expansion.

Appointed Minister to France

His fellow congressmen decided it would be advantageous to send the brilliant Jefferson to Europe to join the team of Benjamin Franklin and John Adams as ministers plenipotentiary in negotiating commercial trade agreements for the new nation with England, France, Spain and other countries.

Jefferson was glad to accept the assignment. He resigned from Congress on May 11, 1784, returned to Monticello with Patsy, and began preparations for what turned out to be a five-year mission abroad. He decided to take Patsy with him. They, with two servants, sailed out of Boston Harbor on July 5, 1784 and arrived in Paris, his new headquarters, on August 6. By the following March Franklin had retired from his post of U. S. Minister to France and Jefferson was appointed his successor.

Although most of his time was spent in Paris he took trips to other areas of France, also to England, Holland, Germany, and Italy. He maintained luxurious quarters in Paris and entertained lavishly, which he both enjoyed doing and felt was his responsibility as a diplomat. Expenses beyond what the government reimbursed he paid from his own financial resources. Despite his dislike for large cities in general, he found many delightful attractions in Paris, including architectural wonders, beautiful gardens, historic sites, theaters, concerts, operas, colorful cafes and well-stocked bookstores.

Abigail Adams

Before John and Abigail Adams and their family transferred from Paris to London he frequently visited with them, finding comfort in a family setting of which he himself had been deprived since the death of his wife. Although he had vowed not to remarry he took delight in close acquaintance with several women, and most especially with Maria Cosway, who was visiting Paris from London with her husband Richard. Both Cosways were artists. She was also an accomplished musician: a harpist, pianist, singer and composer. At twenty-nine years of age she was exceedingly beautiful and gracious. Jefferson immediately became enamored of her and she of him. From the day they met until she departed for London a month later they were constant companions, sharing the many delights of Paris.

Maria Cosway

They continued their close friendship through frequent correspondence until her return nearly a year later when they resumed an active friendship. At forty-three he was a year younger than her husband, much more attractive and a much more interesting companion. Her husband was shorter than she and had somewhat the appearance of a monkey. But he was talented, wealthy, and unfortunately—he was her husband. Jefferson said that in her company he "felt gloriously alive," and in sorrow at her second departure observed that he was "born to lose everything I love." From her letters it is obvious that Maria had a deep love for Jefferson.

In the American Revolution against England, France had given decisive aid to the colonists, both militarily and financially. A Frenchman particularly helpful was the Marquis de Lafayette, who served as a military aide to Washington. After conclusion of the Revolution he returned to France and worked diligently to effect needed changes in the French government. Under King Louis XVI and Queen Marie Antoinette France was an absolute monarchy and was largely a nation of two classes: the indolent rich and the wretched, hungry poor. It was clear to Lafayette and other patriots that unless some major reforms could be made peacefully there would soon be a revolution.

Lafayette assisted Jefferson as minister to France in various ways and in return sought Jefferson's guidance in his strenuous efforts to introduce policies and measures that would enable Frenchmen to enjoy a satisfactory life. Jefferson was pleased to do that within the restraints of his position as representative of another country. As an observer he daily attended sessions of the French National Assembly where there were heated debates among its members, some favoring the status quo, others seeking limits on the monarchy's powers, still others seeking establishment of a republic such as in America. Jefferson's advice was to change first to a limited monarchy before attempting a republic. He felt the French were not ready for a drastic change.

Although Jefferson had disdain for kings in general he was favorably impressed by a speech King Louis XVI made to the National Assembly. And even though he was readily attracted by beautiful women, of which Marie Antoinette was one, he had a distinct dislike of her. In his autobiography he recorded:

> The King was now become a passive machine in the hands of the National Assembly, and had he been left to himself, he would have willingly acquiesced in whatever they should devise as best for the nation. A wise constitution would have been formed, hereditary in his line, himself placed at its head, with powers so large as to enable him to do all the good of his station, and so limited as to restrain him from its abuse. This he would have faithfully administered, and more than this, I do not believe, he ever wished. But he had a Queen of absolute sway over his weak mind and timid virtue, and of a character the reverse of his in all points. This angel, as gaudily painted in the rhapsodies of [Edmund] Burke, with some smartness of fancy, but no sound sense, was proud, disdainful of restraint, indignant at all obstacles to her will, eager in the pursuit of pleasure, and firm enough to hold to her desires, or perish in their wreck. . . . I have ever believed that, had there been no Queen, there would have been no revolution.

Returns to America

After five years in France Jefferson was anxious to return to America, particularly to Virginia, and more especially to Monticello. Shortly after arriving in France he had received a letter informing him that his youngest child, Lucy Elizabeth, had died, at two years of age. His six-year-old daughter Mary, whom he called Polly, had nearly died at the same time. About three years later he had Polly brought to Paris, leaving home in May, 1787, along with his slave girl Sally Hemings, sister of his servant James, who had accompanied him and Patsy to Paris. En route Polly and Sally stayed several weeks with John and Abigail Adams in London, finally reaching Paris in July. Polly joined Patsy at a convent school in Paris.

One day while traveling by buggy near the royal palace Jefferson saw a citizen mob angrily throwing rocks at German mercenary soldiers guarding the estate. A short time later he received the startling word that several government officials had been captured by the mob and beheaded. The bloody French Revolution had begun. Thousands would die at the guillotine, including Louis XVI and Marie Antoinette. And instead of achieving a republic, the French would slip into a dictatorship under the evil Napoleon Bonaparte, who sought to conquer all of Europe.

Months earlier Jefferson had applied for a leave of absence from his Paris post. Finally permission was granted. He, his two daughters and their three servants left for home aboard the merchant ship Clermont on October 7, 1789, headed for the port of Norfolk, Virginia. It was a pleasant journey. Patsy was now seventeen and Polly eleven. Jefferson desired to get them away from both the dangers of the Revolution and the prevailing immorality in France. He left France with mixed feelings. He estimated that of its twenty million citizens, nineteen million lived wretched lives due to the evils of an absolute monarchy—more wretched than even the slaves in America. Yet in his autobiography written years later he still had fond memories of his five years there:

> A more benevolent people I have never known, nor greater warmth and devotedness in their select friendships. Their kindness and accommodation to strangers is unparalleled, and the hospitality of Paris is beyond anything I had conceived to be practicable in a large city. Their eminence, too, in science, the communicative dispositions of their scientific men, the politeness of the general manners, the ease and vivacity of their conversation, give a charm to their society, to be found nowhere else.

Appointed Secretary of State

George Washington was first elected President of the United States in 1789, the year Jefferson returned from France. John Adams was elected Vice President. Washington requested Jefferson to be his Secretary of State. James Madison, Jefferson's fellow Virginian, closest political ally, and a leader in Congress, urged him to accept. With some reluctance he did so, though his preference was to remain a private citizen at Monticello. He was now forty-six years of age. Washington was fifty-seven and Adams was fifty-four. Washington reminded Jefferson that he too had preferred to retire from public life after serving as President of the Constitutional Convention.

Jefferson's four years as Secretary of State were marked by political controversy in Washington's cabinet, largely between himself as advocate for states' rights and Alexander Hamilton, Secretary of the Treasury and head of the Federalist Party, who advocated a dominant, centralized federal government. Hamilton, twelve years younger than Jefferson, had been Washington's aide-de-camp during much of the Revolutionary War.

Alexander Hamilton

The two men constantly clashed on policy and theory of government. Neither trusted the other. Hamilton favored an intellectual aristocracy, a government controlled by an elitist class. Jefferson favored an agrarian society and government by the common man. He was relentlessly opposed to an all-powerful central government, and feared that it would lead to denial of states' rights and perhaps even to a monarchy.

To combat the growing influence of Hamilton and his Federalist Party Jefferson established the Democratic-Republican Party. Thus it was that America's dominant two-party political system developed. Washington and Adams were both Federalists, although no party labels were used in Washington's two elections, for he was a unanimous choice.

At the close of Washington's first term he was anxious to retire to his estate at Mount Vernon. But Jefferson, Hamilton and other leaders persuaded him to accept a second four-year term for the good of the country, which was plagued with many problems, both internal and external, including war threats from both England and France.

Hamilton's political views found favor with Washington and Adams. Partly for the sake of harmony in Washington's cabinet Jefferson resigned at the end of the first term and retired once again to Monticello, determined to never leave it again for public office.

At Monticello Jefferson attempted to isolate himself from politics, even declining to subscribe to any newspapers. For

three years he spent most of his time actively engaged in agriculture. He experimented with various crops, for instance, substituting alfalfa and grain for tobacco. He tinkered with various gadgets, inventing some additional conveniences for his house.

Clock (above, far left) operated by a set of cannon balls (left) whose slow descent marked the days. Affixed high up on the wall the clock was reached for winding by a collapsible ladder (far left). All were made to Jefferson's specifications.

The shaft of the weathervane (above, left) was connected to a dial (left) affixed to the ceiling of the enclosed porch. This enabled Jefferson to make observation of wind drift while staying indoors. Above, right is a dumbwaiter located in a panel to the side of his fireplace that Jefferson invented to bring wine from his cellar.

Elected Vice President

But as the national elections of 1796 neared, Madison, Monroe and others urged him to seek the presidency as candidate of the Democratic-Republican Party. Again with considerable reluctance, he agreed to do so. Although he received the greater popular vote, he lost the election to his old friend Federalist John Adams in the Electoral College vote, sixty-eight to seventy-one. As second-high man in the balloting, he became the Vice President under the election rules then in force. The Federalists also controlled Congress, making Jefferson's role as Vice President doubly difficult.

From the French Revolution Napoleon Bonaparte had emerged as a military dictator, much to Jefferson's disgust and keen disappointment. Napoleon's policies brought France and the United States to the brink of war. In the hysteria thus created Congress passed the "Alien and Sedition Acts" designed to crush all political opposition through fines, imprisonment and even deportation of aliens within the confines of the United States.

Jefferson was horrified by their passage, regarding them as unconstitutional and a suppression of freedom of speech, freedom of the press and freedom of political opposition. He and Madison drafted Resolutions for the states of Kentucky and Virginia, declaring States Rights doctrines that pitted the states against any federal laws considered by them to be unconstitutional.

(Sixty years later, the Southern Confederacy cited these Resolutions in support of the right to secede from the Union. Jefferson's namesake, Jefferson Davis, became the Confederate President and Thomas Jefferson's grandson, George Wythe Randolph, became the Confederate Secretary of War.)

Charles C. Pinckney

Having barely missed attaining the presidency in 1796 Jefferson decided to try for it in 1800. By now there were sixteen states in the Union. The Federalists sought the reelection of President John Adams and as Vice President Charles Pinckney of South Carolina. The Democrat-Republicans ran Jefferson for President and Aaron Burr of New York as Vice President. Burr had been Attorney-General in Washington's first cabinet, then a U. S. Senator. Each member of the Electoral College was entitled to cast votes for two individuals. The results were: Jefferson and Burr each seventy-three votes; Adams, sixty-five, Pinckney, sixty-four, and John Jay, one.

Although Jefferson and Burr had won election, the rules were such that because Burr had received as many votes as Jefferson, the House of Representatives had to break

Aaron Burr

the tie between them to determine which man would be President and which Vice President. Had Burr been honorable he would have acknowledged Jefferson as President, as was the intent of their party. But he and the Federalist enemies of Jefferson saw the possibility of placing Burr in the presidency and causing Jefferson to continue as Vice President.

In the House of Representatives each state would have one vote, its vote to be decided by a majority of its representatives in the House. To win the presidency Jefferson or Burr had to get the vote of at least nine of the sixteen states. On the first ballot Jefferson won the vote of eight states; Burr, six, while two states abstained from voting, being unable to reconcile differences within their delegations. By individual vote counts within the various delegations Burr led Jefferson fifty-five to fifty-one.

Elected President

Alexander Hamilton, who had resigned from Washington's cabinet two years after Jefferson had, was still a powerful leader of the Federalist Party. He and Burr were both New Yorkers. Hamilton still hated Jefferson, but he also hated Burr, so he broke with other Federalists and used his influence to keep New York's delegation in support of Jefferson, "with whose principles I disagree" rather than Burr, "who has no principles." After thirty-five ballots cast over four days (including a Sunday recess), two states on the thirty-sixth ballot switched to Jefferson, giving him the majority he needed for the presidency. Burr became the Vice President.

On the morning of March 4, 1801, Jefferson in company with several friends strode from his boarding house to the north wing of the Capitol building, the only portion completed, where as Vice President he had presided over the Senate.

Flanked by Aaron Burr on his right and Chief Justice John Marshall on his left, he delivered his inaugural address to a joint session of the Senate and House of Representatives.

President John Adams, bitter over his defeat for reelection, disillusioned with politics, and sorrowing over the recent death of his wayward son Charles, had not bothered to stay for the inauguration. He left before dawn that morning to return to his home in Massachusetts. For eleven years he and Jefferson had no communication with each other.

Following his inaugural speech, which was conciliatory in tone in an effort to pacify the Federalists, Jefferson at nearly

John Marshall

fifty-eight years of age took the oath of office, administered by fellow Virginian and kinsman Marshall, a staunch Federalist whom Adams had earlier appointed Secretary of State and just before leaving office had appointed Chief Justice to counter Jefferson's influence as President.

Jefferson was the first President to be inaugurated in Washington, D. C., the new capital on the Potomac, whose location and design he had influenced.

Purchases Louisiana Territory

Of Jefferson's several achievements as President, his greatest was the Louisiana Purchase. In 1803 Napoleon, strapped for war funds, offered to sell France's entire Louisiana Territory, the middle third of what is now the United States, to Jefferson for fifteen million dollars. Even though its purchase violated the Constitution, it was too good an offer to pass up. It would not only double the geographic size of the United States, it would get rid of another foreign power from the North American continent and thus help secure America's future. This tract of land totalled eight hundred thousand square miles, from the Mississippi River to the Rocky Mountains. It included all or portions of the present day states of Colorado, Wyoming, Montana, New Mexico, Louisiana, Arkansas, Missouri, Iowa, Minnesota, North Dakota, South Dakota, Nebraska, Kansas, Oklahoma, and Texas. Obviously the Native Americans who lived in this vast area were not consulted on the sale and purchase of their land and their homes.

While Jefferson was President, his daughter Polly, married in 1797 to John Wayles Eppes, died on April 17, 1804, at twenty-five years of age. His daughter Patsy, who had married her cousin Thomas Mann Randolph Jr. in 1790, was now Jefferson's sole surviving child.

Later, in 1804, Jefferson was easily elected to a second term as President. So popular had his administration been that he received all but fourteen of the one hundred and seventy-six electoral votes. His Federalist opponent was the same Charles C. Pinckney of South Carolina who had been John Adams' vice presidential candidate four years earlier. George Clinton of New York became Jefferson's Vice President, replacing Aaron Burr. There had been no love nor trust between Jefferson and Burr since the 1801 election when Burr let himself become the tool of the Federalists in their attempt to deny Jefferson the presidency.

In 1804 Burr ran for Governor of New York. When Hamilton helped to defeat him, as he had four years earlier for the presidency, Burr's anger against Hamilton became so intense that he challenged him to a pistol duel and killed him. Shortly afterward, he began scheming to establish an empire in the land gained by the Louisiana Purchase, to set himself upon the "throne of the Montezumas." In 1807, Jefferson had him arrested on charges of treason and brought him to trial in Richmond. Chief Justice John Marshall, Jefferson's political enemy, presided at the trial. In his charge to the jury he gave a narrow definition of treason and Burr was acquitted. Burr returned to his law practice in New York.

Much of Jefferson's second term was spent in a struggle to keep America free from entanglements with England, France and Spain. Napoleon was attempting to conquer all of Europe and England was attempting to rule supreme on the seas. They were at war with each other. Jefferson's policy was to steer clear of them. To his political ally and fellow Virginian James Monroe he stated:

> I have ever deemed it fundamental for the United States never to take active part in the quarrels of Europe. Their political interests are entirely distinct from ours. Their mutual jealousies, their balance of power, their complicated alliances, their forms and principles of government, are all foreign to us. They are nations of eternal war.

It is unfortunate that other presidents have not heeded that wise counsel.

Retires to Monticello

Upon completion of his second term in March, 1809, Jefferson was pleased to turn the presidency over to his dear friend James Madison and retire to private life at his beloved estate of Monticello. Those must have been lonely years for him, with nearly all of his family gone. Yet he stayed active in farming and other interests. He maintained an extensive correspondence, had numerous visitors, and kept in touch with Madison, Monroe and other political friends. Through correspondence he even resumed his friendship with John Adams, living in Massachusetts. More than a hundred and fifty letters passed between them.

In June of 1812 English forces again invaded America. They sacked Washington, D. C., and burned the Library of Congress. To help restock it, and to ameliorate his own precarious financial condition, Jefferson sold several hundred of his choice books.

In 1814, as the war with England began winding down, Jefferson again drafted a bill, much as the one he had in 1779, to establish a state-supported system of free public education.

One of his last acts of public service was establishing the University of Virginia on two hundred and fifty acres at nearby Charlottesville, over a period of nine years, from 1816 to 1825. He raised funding for it through private donations and legislative appropriations. He designed the campus and the buildings and supervised their construction. He planned its curriculum and recruited its faculty. He compiled a list of thousands of books for its library and selected the reading for some of its courses.

He did all of this despite his failing health while he was in his seventies and early eighties. The University opened its doors to students in 1825, the year before Jefferson's death. He referred to it as "the last of my mortal cares and the last service I can render to my country." It was one of the three achievements he requested be mentioned on his tombstone.

IV
A Religious Revolution

T he American Revolution against England is generally thought of as a political revolution—a revolt against the despotic abuse of authority by a Whig oligarchy in Parliament and by England's King George III, who eventually became insane. And of course it was a political revolution.

But we should remember that it was also a religious revolution, for it successfully defied the age-old, vicious doctrine of the Divine Right of Kings.

For centuries millions of people throughout the world had suffered oppression, injustices and poverty under the tyranny of kings, whom they had been taught to believe were divinely appointed—designated by God—to rule over them, and to rule them as they pleased.

It was Thomas Jefferson who, in denouncing the Divine Right of Kings, declared:

> We hold these truths to be self-evident, that all men are created equal; that they are endowed by their Creator with inherent and inalienable rights, that among these are life, liberty, and the pursuit of happiness.[6]

Kings, he was saying, have no special, divine attributes or rights making them the superior of others. And in fact there

---

6. Declaration of Independence.

should be no kings, no such leeches on society. To most of the world that was a new and dangerous idea.

"All eyes are opened, or opening, to the rights of man," wrote Jefferson in 1826, the year of his death, fifty years after penning the Declaration of Independence.

> The general spread of the light of science has already laid open to every view the palpable truth, that the mass of mankind has not been born with saddles on their backs, nor a favored few booted and spurred, ready to ride them legitimately by the grace of God.[7]

Jefferson's contempt for kings was forcefully stated in a letter in 1810 in which he noted:

> The practice of kings marrying only in the families of kings, has been that of Europe for some centuries. Now, take any race of animals, confine them in idleness and inaction, whether in a stye, a stable or a stateroom, pamper them with high diet, gratify all their sexual appetites, immerse them in sensualities, nourish their passions, let everything bend before them, and banish whatever might lead them to think, and in a few generations they become all body and no mind. . . . Such is the regimen in raising kings, and in this way they have gone on for centuries.

> While in Europe, [as U.S. Minister to France] I often amused myself with contemplating the characters of the then reigning sovereigns . . . Louis XVI [of France] was a fool, of my own knowledge . . . The King of Spain [Charles IV] was a fool, and of Naples [Ferdinand IV] the same. They passed their lives in hunting, and dispatched two couriers a week, one thousand miles, to let each other know what game they had killed the preceding days. The King of Sardinia [Victor Amadeus III] was a fool. All these were Bourbons. The Queen of Portugal [the Mad Maria], a Braganza, was an idiot by nature. And so was the King of Denmark [Christian VII]. . . .

---

7. Letter to Weightman, June 24, 1826, ten days before Jefferson's death.

The King of Prussia [Frederick William II], . . . was a mere hog in body as well as in mind. Gustavus [III] of Sweden, and Joseph [II] of Austria, were really crazy, and George [III] of England, you know, was in a straight waistcoat [strait jacket, to restrain him from violence due to mental derangement]. . . . These animals had become without mind and powerless; and so will every hereditary monarch be after a few generations. . . . And so endeth the Book of Kings, from all of whom the Lord deliver us.[8]

These delightful observations were expressed in 1810, a year after Jefferson had completed two terms as President of the United States and retired to his beloved estate of Monticello, with time to reflect on the past. Twenty-three years earlier, in 1787, he had also expressed his contempt for kings in a series of letters. In one of those letters he refers to them as "human lions, tigers, and mammoths" and cautions wealthy Americans against marrying kings' "nieces, sisters, etc."[9] In another he says, "No race of kings has ever presented above [more than] one man of common sense in twenty generations."[10] And this: "With all the defects of our [U. S.] constitution . . . the comparison of our government with those of Europe is like a comparison of heaven and hell."[11]

While serving as America's Minister to France Jefferson wrote to President George Washington, in whose cabinet he would soon serve as Secretary of State:

> I was much an enemy to monarchies before I came to Europe. I am ten thousand times more so, since I have seen what they are.
>
> There is scarcely an evil known in these [European] countries which may not be traced to their kings . . . There is not a crowned head in Europe, whose talents or merits would

---

8. Letter to J. Langdon, 1810.
9. Letter to Hawkins, 1787.
10. Letter to Hawkins, 1787.
11. Letter to Joseph Jones, 1787.

entitle him to be elected a vestryman by the people of any parish in America.[12]

His view of kings is in harmony with that of Jehovah Himself, who warned the Israelites against having kings, and saw them suffer under one rotten king after another, with but rare exceptions.

One of Jefferson's fond hopes was that other nations would be inspired by America's example of achieving political and religious freedom:

> Convinced that the republican is the only form of government which is not eternally at open or secret war with the rights of mankind, my prayers and efforts shall be cordially distributed to the support of that [which] we have so happily established. It is indeed an animating thought, that while we are securing the rights of ourselves and our posterity, we are pointing out the way to struggling nations, who wish like us to emerge from their tyrannies also.[13]

Inasmuch as the mission of the LDS Church is worldwide, to take the Restored Gospel of Jesus Christ to "every nation, kindred, tongue and people," Jefferson's hope for the "struggling nations" to "emerge from their tyrannies" through America's example was a most timely desire for him to have as a forerunner to the Prophet.

---

12. Letter to Washington, 1788.
13. Letter to Hunter, 1790.

V
Beware of the Judiciary

How extremely important were the American Revolution and the establishment of a republican-democratic form of government as preliminary steps to the Restoration of the Gospel of Jesus Christ upon the earth! A basic doctrine of the true church, a doctrine dating back to the Grand Council in Heaven when Lucifer was cast out, is that man should exercise his free agency. And that is most fully possible, of course, only under a republican-democratic form of government, where people are free.

So we see the tremendous importance of the role that Jefferson played in the divine plan.

Even after our Republic was founded there were people, especially some of the military leaders, who desired to revert back to some form of government other than a republic or democracy. Several influential men, including a coterie of army officers, urged George Washington to become a king—a suggestion that he quickly and emphatically rejected.

Jefferson, of course, was opposed to such a notion, and opposed also to the Federalist Party view of a strong central government at the expense of individual states' rights. He took the lead in establishing the Republican-Democratic Party to battle for freedom from an overly powerful federal government. To a friend he wrote in 1821:

To this I am opposed because, when all government, domestic and foreign, in little as in great things, shall be drawn to Washington as the center of all power, it will render powerless the checks provided of one government or another, and will become as venal and oppressive as the government [England] from which we separated.

One of his gravest concerns was the misbehavior of the federal judiciary and especially the practice of giving lifetime appointments to members of the Supreme Court and to other federal judges, which he feared would lead to a "despotism of an oligarchy." He urged that judges be appointed for six years only, rather than for life. Obviously the inept American judicial system from which society suffers today would be in much better condition if Jefferson's suggestion had been followed.

VI
Statute for Religious Freedom

It was Jefferson who led the fight for separation of Church and State—that "loathsome combination," as he called it, which continues even today in many European, Mideastern, Russian and other countries of the world, where official state religions rob their people of true religious freedom and force them through taxation to support religions not of their choice.

In 1777, Jefferson penned his famous "Act for Establishing Religious Freedom," which was eventually passed in the Assembly of Virginia in 1786 as the *Statute of Virginia for Religious Freedom*—one of the three deeds Jefferson wished to have included in his epitaph. It is well worth reading this Act carefully:

> Well aware that Almighty God hath created the mind free.
>
> That all attempts to influence it by temporal punishments or burdens, or by civil incapacitations, tend only to beget habits of hypocrisy and meanness, and are a departure from the plan of the Holy Author of our religion, who being Lord both of body and mind, yet chose not to propagate it by coercions on either, as was in his Almighty power to do.
>
> That the impious presumption of legislators and rulers, civil as well as ecclesiastical, who, being themselves but fallible and uninspired men, have assumed dominion over the faith of others, setting up their own opinions and modes of

thinking as the only true and infallible, and as such endeavoring to impose them on others, hath established and maintained false religions over the greatest part of the world, and through all time.

That to compel a man to furnish contributions of money for the propagation of opinions which he disbelieves, is sinful and tyrannical.

That even the forcing him to support this or that teacher of his own religious persuasion, is depriving him of the comfortable liberty of giving his contributions to the particular pastor whose morals he would make his pattern, and whose powers he feels most persuasive to righteousness, and is withdrawing from the ministry those temporal rewards, which proceeding from an approbation of their personal conduct, are an additional incitement to earnest and unremitting labors for the instruction of mankind;

That our civil rights have no dependence on our religious opinions, [any] more than our opinions in physics or geometry;

That, therefore, the proscribing any citizen as unworthy the public confidence by laying upon him an incapacity of being called to the offices of trust and emolument, unless he profess or renounce this or that religious opinion, is depriving him injuriously of those privileges and advantages to which in common with his fellow citizens he has a natural right;

That it tends also to corrupt the principles of that very religion it is meant to encourage, by bribing, with a monopoly of worldly honors and emoluments, those who will externally profess and conform to it;

That though indeed these are criminal who do not withstand such temptation, yet neither are those innocent who lay the bait in their way;

That to suffer the civil magistrate to intrude his powers into the field of opinion and to restrain the profession or propagation of principles, on the supposition of their ill tendency, is a dangerous fallacy, which at once destroys all religious liberty, because he being of course judge of that tendency, will make his opinions the rule of judgment, and approve or condemn the sentiments of others only as they shall square with or differ from his own;

That it is time enough for the rightful purposes of civil government, for its offices to interfere when principles break out into overt acts against peace and good order;

And finally, that truth is great and will prevail if left to herself; that she is the proper and sufficient antagonist to error, and has nothing to fear from the conflict, unless by human interposition disarmed of her natural weapons, free argument and debate, errors ceasing to be dangerous when it is permitted freely to contradict them.

Be it therefore enacted by the General Assembly, That no man shall be compelled to frequent or support any religious worship, place or ministry whatsoever, nor shall be enforced, restrained, molested, or burthened in his body or goods, nor shall otherwise suffer on account of his religious opinions or belief; but that all men shall be free to profess, and by argument to maintain, their opinions in matters of religion, and that the same shall in nowise diminish, enlarge, or affect their civil capacities.

. . . we are free to declare, and do declare, that the rights hereby asserted are of the natural rights of mankind, and that if any act shall be hereafter passed to repeal the present or to narrow its operation, such act will be an infringement of natural right.

Nor was Jefferson content to have this separation of Church and State safeguarded in Virginia alone. Copies of this Act were quickly distributed throughout the United States and Europe.

"Our act for freedom of religion is extremely applauded," Jefferson wrote to his friend and teacher, George Wythe, in 1786, the year of its passage. He continued,

"The ambassadors and ministers of the several nations of Europe, resident at this court [Jefferson was then in Paris, as U.S. Minister to France], have asked of me copies of it, to send to their sovereigns, and it is inserted at full length in several books now in the press. . . . I think it will produce considerable good even in these [European] countries, where ignorance, superstition, poverty, and oppression of body and mind, in every form, are so firmly settled on the mass of the people, that their redemption from them can never be hoped. . . ."

Little wonder that the clergymen were bitter against Jefferson and indulged in a smear campaign against him, for by the passage of this Act he foiled, at least in America, their age-old practice of feeding at the tax-supported public trough, securing power and wealth to themselves by mixing religion with politics, combining Church with State, for personal profit and prestige.

"The clergy," Jefferson later wrote, "by getting themselves established by law and engrafted into the machine of government, have been a very formidable engine against the civil and religious rights of man."[14]

"In every country and in every age, the priest has been hostile to liberty. He is always in alliance with the despot, abetting his abuses in return for protection of his own."[15]

James Madison

"History, I believe, furnishes no example of a priest-ridden people maintaining a free civil government."[16]

Jefferson was serving as U.S. Minister to France at the time the U.S. Constitution was being framed. Upon reading the completed document he wrote to his friend James Madison, who would later succeed him as President of the United States:

---

14. Letter to J. Moor, 1800.
15. Letter to Horatio G. Spafford, 1814.
16. Letter to Baron Von Humboldt, 1813.

. . . I will now tell you what I do not like [about the Constitution]. First, the omission of a bill of rights, providing clearly, and without the aid of sophism, for freedom of religion, freedom of the press, protection against standing armies. . . .

A bill of rights is what the people are entitled to against every government on earth, general or particular; and what no just government should refuse, or rest on inference.

Two years later, in 1789, the first ten amendments to the Constitution, known as the Bill of Rights, were introduced, prepared chiefly by Madison, under Jefferson's influence and guidance. These were adopted before the close of 1791.

To Jefferson's satisfaction, and credit, the first Bill of Rights, or amendment, states:

Congress shall make no law respecting an establishment of religion, or prohibiting the free exercise thereof; or abridging the freedom of speech, or of the press; or the right of the people peaceably to assemble, and to petition the government for redress of grievances.

Thus Jefferson was instrumental in securing in the new Republic a separation of Church and State, so vital to religious freedom and true democracy.

Throughout his long life—he lived to the age of eighty-three—Jefferson continued to champion the cause of religious freedom. Typical of his many declarations was this letter to Edward Dowse in 1803 in which he said:

I never will, by any word or act, bow to the shrine of intolerance, or admit a right of inquiry into the religious opinions of others. On the contrary, we are bound, you, I, and every one, to make common cause, even with error itself, to maintain the common right of freedom of conscience. We ought with one heart and one hand to hew down the daring and dangerous efforts of those who would seduce the public opinion to substitute itself into . . . tyranny over religious faith.

The Prophet Joseph Smith—continually persecuted by church ministers who chose to make a mockery of the Bill of Rights as well as the teachings of Christ—reiterated Jefferson's principles when in 1842 he declared in the LDS Articles of Faith:

> We claim the privilege of worshipping Almighty God according to the dictates of our own conscience, and allow all men the same privilege, let them worship how, where or what they may."[17]

The Prophet Joseph Smith

---

17. Article of Faith number 11, in the Pearl of Great Price.

VII

Close Agreement on Views

I s it not reasonable to expect that men inspired of God to accomplish His purposes should hold the same general views? There is a striking similarity in Thomas Jefferson's and Joseph Smith's philosophies on government, education, and religion.

Although the Prophet is thought of primarily as a religious leader, he was also a great statesman, one of the greatest ever. His *Views On The Powers And Policy Of Government*, issued when he was seeking the presidency of the United States in 1844, is a masterpiece in political thought. Had he been elected instead of assassinated, the United States could likely have been spared the Civil War.

In the *Book of Mormon*, in the *Doctrine and Covenants*, and in the *Pearl of Great Price* there are many references to things political. One entire section of the D&C, section 134, is "A Declaration of Belief regarding Governments and Laws in general." To quote briefly from this document:

> We believe that governments were instituted of God for the benefit of man; and that he holds men accountable for their acts in relation to them, both in making laws and administering them, for the good and safety of society.

We believe that no government can exist in peace, except such laws are framed and held inviolate as will secure to each individual the free exercise of conscience, the right and control of property, and the protection of life. . . .

We believe that religion is instituted of God; and that men are amenable to him, and to him only, for the exercise of it, unless their religious opinions prompt them to infringe upon the rights and liberties of others; but we do not believe that human law has a right to interfere in prescribing rules of worship to bind the consciences of men, nor dictate forms for public or private devotion; that the civil magistrate should restrain crime, but never control conscience; should punish guilt, but never suppress the freedom of the soul. . . .

We do not believe it just to mingle religious influence with civil government, whereby one religious society is fostered and another proscribed in its spiritual privileges, and the individual rights of its members, as citizens, denied. . . .

Compare that, and the Prophet's other political views, to those of Jefferson, and note how alike the two men thought. Consider a few typical statements by Jefferson:

I know of no safe depository of the ultimate powers of the society but the people themselves.[18]

The true foundation of republican government is the equal right of every citizen, in his person and property, and in their management.[19]

Every man, and every body of men on earth, possesses the right of self-government.[20]

Sometimes it is said that man cannot be trusted with the government of himself. *Can he, then, be trusted with the government of others?* Or have we found angels in the form of kings to govern him?[21]

---

18. Letter to Jarvis, 1821.
19. Letter to Samuel Kercheval, 1816.
20. Political statement by Jefferson in 1790 regarding the seat of government.
21. Jefferson's First Inaugural Address, March 4, 1801.

All, too, will bear in mind this sacred principle, that though the will of the majority is in all cases to prevail, that will, to be rightful, must be reasonable; that the minority possess their equal rights, which equal laws must protect, and to violate which would be oppression. . . .[22]

Is it not a safe assumption that had Jefferson been President of the United States during the early years of the LDS Church, the Saints would never have suffered, at least not without redress, the bitter persecutions that they endured during the administrations of such mediocre presidents as Martin Van Buren, James Buchanan and others?

Jefferson Memorial in Washington, D.C.,
dedicated in 1943 to the memory of Thomas Jefferson.
A white marble structure in classical style, designed by John Russell Pope
and contains a statue of Jefferson by Rudolph Evans.

---

22. Jefferson's First Inaugural Address, March 4, 1801.

VIII

"I Have Sworn Upon the Altar of God"

Now let us compare further Thomas Jefferson's and Joseph Smith's views on religion:

Like the Prophet a generation later, Jefferson was bitterly assailed in the press and from the pulpit. Probably no two men in American history have been more vilified during their lifetime. A good indication, is it not, of the efforts of Satan, stirring up the people against the servants of God, such as has been the case throughout the long history of mankind?

Jefferson was so viciously assailed by the political and sectarian newspapers of his day that he chose to express most of his views in hundreds of private letters rather than through the press.

A majority of the most frenzied persecutors of both Jefferson and Joseph Smith were the "religious" leaders of the day: church ministers.

On the beautiful Jefferson Memorial in Washington, D.C., are inscribed these immortal words of his:

"I have sworn upon the altar of God, eternal hostility against every form of tyranny over the mind of man."

This statement is always given a political implication or connotation. But the truth is, Jefferson was referring particularly to the churches of his day. The ministers and priests and rabbis professed to believe that he was an atheist and an infidel. They so labeled him, creating a falsehood that persists even today. They were angry with him because he successfully fought to keep them from being on the public payroll, and from having state-sponsored churches.

Jefferson's statement was made in a letter he wrote to his friend Dr. Benjamin Rush in the year 1800, the year he was elected president. The more complete statement, so far as pertinent to the subject, is this:

Benjamin Rush

> They [the clergy] believe that any portion of power confided to me, will be exerted in opposition to their schemes. And they believe rightly: for I have sworn upon the altar of God, eternal hostility against every form of tyranny over the mind of man. But this is all they have to fear from me: and enough too in their opinion.

In the Prophet Joseph's autobiographical sketch, as recorded in the *Pearl of Great Price*, he reports:

Some time in the second year after our [Joseph's parents' family] removal to Manchester [New York], there was in the place where we lived an unusual excitement on the subject of religion. It commenced with the Methodists, but soon became general among all the sects in that region. Indeed, the whole district seemed affected by it, and great multitudes united themselves to the different religious parties, which created no small stir and division amongst the people, some crying, 'Lo here!' and others, 'Lo there!' Some were contending for the Methodist faith, some for the Presbyterian, and some for the Baptist.

For notwithstanding the great love which the converts to these different faiths expressed at the time of their conversion, and the great zeal manifested by the respective clergy, who were active in getting up and promoting this extraordinary scene of religious feelings, in order to have everybody converted, as they were pleased to call it, let them join what sect they pleased—yet when the converts began to file off, some to one party and some to another, it was seen that the seemingly good feeling of both the priests and the converts were more pretended than real, for a scene of great confusion and bad feeling ensued, priest contending against priest and convert against convert, so that all good feelings one for another, if they ever had any, were entirely lost in the strife of words and a contest about opinions.

I was at this time in my fifteenth year. . . . In the midst of this war of words and tumult of opinions, I often said to myself: What is to be done? Who of all these parties are right; or, are they all wrong together? If any one of them be right, which is it, and how shall I know it?

While I was laboring under the extreme difficulties caused by the contests of these parties of religionists, I was one day reading the Epistle of James, first chapter and fifth verse, which reads: If any of you lack wisdom, let him ask of God, that giveth to all men liberally, and upbraideth not; and it shall be given him.

Never did any passage of scripture come with more power to the heart of man than this did at this time to mine. It seemed to enter with great force into every feeling of my heart. I reflected on it again and again, knowing that if any person needed wisdom from God, I did; for how to act I did not know, and unless I could get more wisdom than I then had, I would never know; for the teachers of religion of the different sects understood the same passages of scripture so differently as to destroy all confidence in settling the question by an appeal to the Bible.

At length I came to the conclusion that I must either remain in darkness and confusion, or else I must do as James directs, that is, ask of God. I at length came to the determination to 'ask of God,' concluding that if he gave wisdom to them that lacked wisdom, and would give liberally, and not upbraid, I might venture. . . .

Then the Prophet goes on to tell of how he sought divine guidance and received a glorious vision of God the Father and the Son. And of the instructions he received from Jesus Christ at this time, he writes:

> I was answered that I must join none of them [none of the churches], for they were all wrong, and the Personage who addressed me said that all their creeds were an abomination in His sight, that those professors were all corrupt; that 'they draw near to me with their lips, but their hearts are far from me, they teach for doctrines the commandments of men, having a form of godliness, but they deny the power thereof.'. . .

> Some few days after I had this vision, I happened to be in company with one of the Methodist preachers, who was very active in the before mentioned religious excitement, and, conversing with him on the subject of religion, I took occasion to give him an account of the vision which I had had. I was greatly surprised at his behavior; he treated my communication not only lightly, but with great contempt, saying it was all of the devil, that there were no such things as visions or revelations in these days, that all such things had ceased with the apostles, and that there would never be any more of them.

> I soon found, however, that my telling the story had excited a great deal of prejudice against me among professors of religion, and was the cause of great persecution, which continued to increase; and though I was an obscure boy, only between fourteen and fifteen years of age, and my circumstances in life such as to make a boy of no consequence in the world, yet men of high standing would take notice sufficient to excite a bitter persecution; and this was common among all the sects—all united to persecute me. . . .

Now compare these statements of the Prophet Joseph with those of Jefferson as expressed in some letters written at approximately this same time. In a letter to H. G. Spafford in 1816 he wrote:

> I am not afraid of the priests. They have tried upon me all their various batteries, of pious whining, hypocritical canting, lying and slandering, without being able to give me one moment of pain. . . . Their sway in New England is indeed formidable. No mind beyond mediocrity dares there to develop itself.

And from his letter in 1815 to Dr. Benjamin Waterhouse:

> The priests have so disfigured the simple religion of Jesus that no one who reads the sophistications they have engrafted on it, from the jargon of Plato, of Aristotle and other mystics, would conceive these could have been fathered [by] the sublime preacher of the Sermon on the Mount. Yet, knowing the importance of names, they have assumed that of Christians, while they are mere Platonists, or anything rather than disciples of Jesus.

And to Samuel Kercheval in 1810, Jefferson wrote:

> But a short time elapsed after the death of the great reformer of the Jewish religion, before his principles were departed from by those who professed to be his special servants, and perverted into an engine for enslaving mankind, and aggrandizing their oppressors in Church and State: that the purest system of morals ever before preached to man has been adulterated and sophisticated by artificial constructions, into a mere contrivance to filch wealth and power to themselves: that rational men, not being able to swallow their impious heresies, in order to force them down their throats, they raise the hue and cry of infidelity, while themselves are the greatest obstacles to the advancement of the real doctrines of Jesus, and do, in fact, constitute the real Anti-Christ.

Other typical statements by Jefferson include these:

I know [my statements] will give great offense to the New England clergy; but the advocate of religious freedom is to expect neither peace nor forgiveness from them.[23]

The sum of all religion as expressed by its best preacher, 'Fear God and love thy neighbor', contains no mystery, needs no explanation. But this won't do. It gives no scope to make dupes; priests could not live by it.[24]

Our Savior did not come into this world to save metaphysicians only. His doctrines are levelled to the simplest understanding, and it is only by banishing Hierophantic mysteries and Scholastic subtleties, which they have nicknamed Christianity, and getting back to the plain and unsophisticated precepts of Christ, that we become *real* Christians.[25]

It is too late in the day for men of sincerity to pretend they believe in the Platonic mysticisms that three are one, and one is three; and yet that the one is not three, and the three are not one. . . . But this constitutes the craft, the power and the profit of the priests. Sweep away their gossamer fabrics of fictitious religion, and they would catch no more flies. . . .[26]

Of all the systems of morality, ancient and modern, which have come under my observation, none appear to me so pure as that of Jesus.[27]

Had the doctrines of Jesus been preached always as pure as they came from his lips the whole civilized world would now have been Christian.[28]

I am a Christian, in the only sense in which he wished any one to be; sincerely attached to his doctrines, in preference to all others.[29]

---

23. Letter to Attorney-General Levi Lincoln, 1802.
24. Letter to Logan, 1816.
25. Letter to S. Hales, 1818.
26. Letter to John Adams, 1813.
27. Letter to W. Canby, 1813.
28. Letter to Dr. Benjamin Waterhouse, 1822.
29. Letter to Dr. Benjamin Rush, 1803.

So it is clear that Jefferson's views on the religions of his day compare exactly with those of the Prophet Joseph, who denounced false religions as "the great whore of all the earth."

As Brigham Young, the Prophet's aide, student and successor, expressed it, the priests and their doctrines were "as blind as Egyptian darkness." With this Jefferson agreed. Said he, of sectarian dogma:

> It is the mere abracadabra of the mountebanks calling themselves the priests of Jesus. If it could be understood it would not answer their purpose. Their security is in their faculty of shedding darkness. . . .[30]

The White House, Washington, D.C., official residence of the President, as it appears today. It was Jefferson's residence 1801-1809. He was the first President to occupy it. It was under construction 1792-1801, designed and supervised by James Hoban, with input from Jefferson. Originally it was not white. It has been renovated and added to a number of times.

---

30. Letter to F. A. Van der Kemp, 1816.

IX

The Need for Education

It was to battle against these forces of darkness that Jefferson, like the Prophet Joseph after him, advocated and promoted education, at a time when the masses were illiterate. Ignorance, superstition and fear—the bulwarks of the religions of the day—are of Satan, while knowledge, understanding, wisdom and love are the attributes of the real Gospel of Jesus Christ.

That is why Thomas Jefferson and Joseph Smith were two of the foremost advocates of education. Note the close parallel in their views and actions in this matter:

Referring again to the "religious" creeds of the day, Jefferson declared, "to penetrate and dissipate these clouds of darkness, the general mind must be strengthened by education."

Consider further his views on education:

> No one more sincerely wishes the spread of information among mankind than I do, and none has greater confidence in its effect towards supporting free and good government.[31]

> I know of no safe depository of the ultimate powers of the society but the people themselves; and if we think them not enlightened enough to exercise their control with a wholesome discretion, the remedy is not to take it from them, but to inform their discretion by education.[32]

---

31. Letter to Hugh L. White, et al., 1810.
32. Letter to Jarvis, 1821.

If a nation expects to be ignorant and free, in a state of civilization, it expects what never was and never will be.[33]

I look to the diffusion of light and education as the resource most to be relied on for ameliorating the condition, promoting the virtue, and advancing the happiness of man.[34]

The importance of education in the LDS Church is embodied in such profound statements as these in the writings of the Prophet Joseph Smith:

The glory of God is intelligence, or, in other words, light and truth.[35]

It is impossible for a man to be saved in ignorance.[36]

Whatever principle of intelligence we attain unto in this life, it will rise with us in the resurrection. And if a person gains more knowledge and intelligence in this life through his diligence and obedience than another, he will have so much the advantage in the world to come.[37]

A basic and inspiring doctrine of the LDS Church is that "As man now is, God once was, and as God now is, man may become."

In his prayer of dedication of the Kirtland, Ohio, LDS Temple, in 1836, the thirty-year-old Prophet Joseph implored:

. . . And do thou grant, Holy Father, that all those who shall worship in this house may be taught words of wisdom out of the best books, and that they may seek learning by study, and also by faith, as thou hast said; and that they may grow up in thee, and receive a fullness of the Holy Ghost . . .[38]

---

33. Letter to Colonel Yancey, 1816.
34. Letter to C. C. Blatchly, 1822.
35. *Doctrine and Covenants* 93:36
36. *Doctrine and Covenants* 131:6
37. *Doctrine and Covenants* 130:18-19
38. *Doctrine and Covenants* 109:14-15

Three years earlier he had admonished the Saints to "Study and learn and become acquainted with all good books, and with languages, tongues and people."[39]

Amidst poverty and persecution the Prophet established a "School of the Prophets," employed a language teacher, and sent his assistant Oliver Cowdery east to buy a wagon load of books.

And let it always be remembered that the LDS Church started with a book, the *Book of Mormon*, translated by the Prophet at twenty-four years of age. Despite severe persecution, including mob destruction of the LDS printing plant, the book of *Doctrine and Covenants* soon followed, as did other church publications, including newspapers, all for the edification of the Saints.

The young Prophet constantly encouraged his people to become well educated. What a contrast he was to the ministers of other churches, whose "security is in their faculty of shedding darkness," as Jefferson observed.

Is it any wonder that Mormons lead the entire world in educational standards and achievements today?

How proud and grateful Jefferson would have been to belong to a church that emphasizes education, which teaches that the glory of God is intelligence, and that man can become as God!

How Jefferson would have enjoyed the spirit behind the School of the Prophets, where those young frontiersmen eagerly sought knowledge in every field of learning available to them.

Jefferson, like the Prophet Joseph, was personally interested in a great variety of subjects: history, languages, politics, astronomy, agriculture, architecture, music, etc.

Each was the most profound thinker and the greatest intellect of his day, transforming thoughts and knowledge into words and action, for the benefit of all mankind.

---

39. *Doctrine and Covenants* 90:15

X

Significance of
The Louisiana Purchase

Several specific acts of Jefferson as President of the United States give further evidence of his fore-ordination as a leading personality to help prepare the way for the Prophet Joseph in the Restoration of the Gospel of Jesus Christ.

One of these is his famous Louisiana Purchase.

This nation was founded under divine guidance as a preliminary step to the reestablishment of the true church upon the earth. Yet, the nation which was thus founded included only land in the eastern-most portion of what is now the United States of America. During the first two presidential administrations it remained thus limited. The vast tract of land that now comprises the middle third of our country belonged to the French government, a monarchy turned dictatorship.

But when Jefferson became president he seized upon the opportunity of buying from the notorious war monger Napoleon Bonaparte, for fifteen million dollars, all of the country lying between the Mississippi River and the Rocky Mountains.

To make this purchase Jefferson had to "violate" the Constitution. For this he was assailed by priests, politicians, journalists and financiers, for his "illegal extravagance." But Jefferson did not yield to these negative pressures.

His Louisiana Purchase is of utmost significance to the Restoration of the Gospel, for within the boundaries of the purchase lies Jackson County, Missouri, site of the New Jerusalem, the Center of Zion, and nearby, the true location of the Garden of Eden and Adam-ondi-Ahman, where a Grand Council of the Patriarchs and Prophets is to some day convene.

Surely the Lord in having this nation founded as a step toward the Gospel Restoration would have it include this most important geographic area. So again we see evidence of Jefferson's acting under divine guidance.

In connection with his Louisiana Purchase, Jefferson dispatched the Lewis & Clark Expedition, which explored not only the land he had bought, but the country that lay to the west of it as well. This act of Jefferson's was also important to the LDS Church, for when the Prophet Joseph Smith—and after his martyrdom, Brigham Young—made plans for moving to the Rocky Mountains, reports and maps based originally upon the Lewis & Clark Expedition were of considerable help. Also important, the Expedition helped the United States lay claim to the Pacific West.

XI
Opposition to Slavery

Now let us consider yet another "work" of Jefferson's:

You know well that Satan does all in his evil power to thwart the work of God. It was the Lord's plan that a democratic republic be established upon the American continent, preparatory to the Gospel Restoration.

One of the schemes Satan introduced to thwart this divine plan was the practice of slavery, which secured its ugly grasp upon the land long before our nation was founded. Even the famous Mayflower, which had carried Pilgrims to America in search of religious freedom, was converted into a slave ship!

The hideous practice of slavery was in direct violation, opposition and defiance to God's declaration that America should be a land of freedom.

Eventually this evil practice, introduced under satanic influence, resulted in the bloody Civil War, 1861-65, in which more Americans died than have died in all other wars since the founding of the United States.

For decades the practice of slavery kept the United States from being truly united, and even today its aftermath is still sorely felt in the continuing racial problems in our country.

It is interesting to note that as early as 1769, while a member of the Virginia Legislature, Thomas Jefferson urged the passage of a bill for the emancipation of the slaves.

Nearly a hundred years later Virginia paid dearly for ignoring his pleas for justice, for it was on her soil that so many of the bloodiest battles of the Civil War were fought.

From his early manhood until the day of his death, Jefferson was the foremost advocate of emancipation. For instance, in 1784 Virginia ceded to the national government the area northwest of the Ohio River. In the Continental Congress a Northwest Ordinance was drafted as a plan for governing this territory. Jefferson included in it a provision that would have prohibited slavery after 1800 in this and any other territories the United States might later obtain. To Jefferson's dismay the provision was defeated by one vote. "Thus," he said, "we see the fate of millions of unborn hanging on the tongue of one man, and heaven was silent in that awful moment."

As president he made repeated attempts to have the slaves freed and settled in a country to their own liking. He set the example for other plantation owners by arranging for the freedom of his own slaves and helping them adjust to a free role in our society.

Among the many falsehoods leveled against Jefferson by his enemies, and even perpetuated by character assassins today, is that he favored slavery and had one or more Negro mistresses.

Jefferson was not only deeply concerned about the injustice slavery inflicted on the Blacks but the negative effect it had upon the character of the slave owners:

> The whole commerce between master and slave is a perpetual exercise of the most boisterous passions, the most unremitting despotism on the one part, and degrading submissions on the other. Our children see this, and learn to imitate it; for man is an imitative animal . . . and thus nursed, educated, and daily exercised in tyranny, cannot but be stamped by it with odious peculiarities. . . . With the morals of the [slave holders], their industry also is destroyed. For in a warm climate, no man will labor for himself who can make another

labor for him. . . . And can the liberties of a nation be thought secure when we have removed their only firm basis, a conviction in the minds of the people that these liberties are of the gift of God? That they are not to be violated but with His wrath? Indeed I tremble for my country when I reflect that God is just; that His justice cannot sleep forever.[40]

This degradation in the character and personality of slave holders was bitterly felt by Joseph Smith and the Mormons when they attempted to establish cities in the slave state of Missouri. By and large the Missourians were crude, harsh, depraved, indolent, ignorant, intemperate, intolerant and a murderous people, with little or no sense of justice. Eventually the Mormons were forcibly driven from Missouri under an extermination order issued by the drunken tyrant Governor Lilburn Boggs, resulting in heavy loss of life and property, and a death sentence and six-month imprisonment of the Prophet Joseph Smith and other LDS Church leaders in a cold, filthy, vermin-infested dungeon. Protestant ministers were mob leaders in Missouri.

In a letter to De Meunier in 1786 Jefferson gave vent to his feelings against slavery and slavers:

What a stupendous, what an incomprehensible machine is man! who can endure toil, famine, stripes, imprisonment, and death itself, in vindication of his own liberty, and, the next moment be deaf to all those motives whose power supported him through his trial, and inflict on his fellow men a bondage, one hour of which is fraught with more misery than ages of that which he rose in rebellion to oppose. But we must await, with patience, the workings of an overruling Providence, and hope that that is preparing the deliverance of these, our suffering brethren [slaves]. When the measure of their tears shall be full, when their groans shall have involved heaven itself in darkness, doubtless a God of justice will awaken to their distress.

---

40. Jefferson's "Notes on Virginia," Query 14.

Twenty-eight years later, in 1814, Jefferson wrote:

The love of justice and the love of country plead equally the cause of these people [the slaves], and it is a moral reproach to us that they should have pleaded it so long in vain. Yet the hour of emancipation is advancing, in the march of time.[41]

Like the Prophet Joseph Smith after him, Jefferson proposed that the slaves be bought from their owners by the government, set free, and educated. He also suggested that those who wished to return to their ancestral home in Africa be given financial assistance to do so.

In the year of his death, 1826, six years after the infamous Missouri Compromise (which allowed Missouri to join the Union as a slave state), Jefferson expressed the fear that the slavery issue would tear the nation asunder. And so it happened—the bloody, devastating Civil War started with the rebellion of South Carolina, the very place that Joseph Smith prophesied it would.

---

41. Letter to E. Coles, 1814.

XII
Predicts the Gospel Restoration

Thomas Jefferson was President of the United States when Joseph Smith was born, on December 23, 1805. Jefferson (along with our second president, John Adams) died on the fiftieth anniversary of the signing of the American Declaration of Independence, on the Fourth of July, 1826, when Joseph Smith was twenty years old, three years after Joseph was first visited by the Angel Moroni, and just one year before the Prophet received the *Book of Mormon* plates and commenced the work of translation of this sacred record.

In conclusion, focus your attention upon the year 1820: the year in which Joseph Smith as a boy, fourteen years of age, sought in prayer for guidance as to which church he should join, and received that glorious vision in the Sacred Grove in upstate New York; the vision in which Elohim and Jehovah—God the Father and His Beloved Son Jesus Christ—appeared to him and Jesus told Joseph to join none of the churches, for they were all "an abomination" in His sight; the vision in which he was told that the true church was not upon the earth, but one day would be, and that a great mission awaited him if he lived worthy of it.

Now, in that very same year, 1820, Thomas Jefferson, an elder statesman of our country, a past President of the United

States and the author of the Declaration of Independence, pre-
dicted in a letter to his friend F. A. Van Der Kemp:

> The genuine and simple religion of Jesus will one day be
> restored; such as it was preached and practiced by Himself.
> Very soon after His death it became muffled up in myster-
> ies, and has been ever since kept in concealment from the
> vulgar eye. . . .

If, because of the prejudice and false notions in the world,
or for any other reason, you find it difficult to accept the story,
the mission of God's great Latter-day Prophet, Joseph Smith,
then accept the words, the testimony, of the most brilliant and
illustrious of our American presidents, Thomas Jefferson.

Examine closely this church, The Church of Jesus Christ of
Latter-day Saints, and determine for yourself, through study
and prayer, whether or not "the genuine and simple religion of
Jesus" has been restored to the earth, as a preparatory step to
the Second Coming of the Savior Himself.

Sources

Numerous books have been published on Thomas
Jefferson. I have a personal library of several. One volume that has been especially useful to me in this study
is: *Thomas Jefferson on Democracy. The Living Thoughts of
America's Architect of Freedom*. It was edited by Saul K.
Padover and published in paperback by New American Library
as a Mentor Book and earlier published by D. Appleton-
Century Company in hardback. Mr. Padover's excellent book
contains all the direct quotes from Jefferson's letters and some
other writings which I have included here. He has compiled
them from primary and secondary sources. I am indebted to his
book as a time saver.

Among dozens of books you will find worthwhile in your
pursuit of information on the life of Thomas Jefferson are
these:

Dewey, John. *The Living Thoughts of Thomas Jefferson*. New
York: Fawcett Publications, Inc., 1957.
Garrett, Wendell D. *The Worlds of Thomas Jefferson*. New
York: Weathervane Books, 1971.
Koch, Adrienne, and William Peden, eds. *The Life and Selected
Writings of Thomas Jefferson*. New York: Random House,
Modern Library, 1944.
Langguth, A.J. *Patriots: The Men Who Started the American
Revolution*. New York: Simon and Schuster, 1988.
Mapp, Alf J., Jr., *Thomas Jefferson: A Strange Case of
Mistaken Identity*. Lanham: Madison Books, 1987.
Martin, Edwin T. *Thomas Jefferson: Scientist*. New York:
Henry Schuman, Inc., 1952.

Morse, John T., Jr., ed. *Thomas Jefferson*. Boston and New York: Houghton, Mifflin and Company, 1898.

Mott, Frank L. *Jefferson and the Press*. Baton Rouge: Louisiana State University Press, 1943.

Murphy, James M., ed. *Thomas Jefferson*. New York: The Young People's Library of Historical Briefs, 1975.

Padover, Saul K., ed. *Thomas Jefferson on Democracy*. New York: Mentor Books, Appleton-Century Co., Inc., 1954.

Van der Linden, Frank. *The Turning Point: Jefferson's Battle for the Presidency*. New York: Van Rees Press, 1962.

The LDS References Cited Are:

Journal of Discourses, Volume 19. Salt Lake City: The Church of Jesus Christ of Latter-Day Saints.

Lundwall, N. B. *The Vision*. Salt Lake City: Bookcraft. Publication date not stated.

Report of General Conference, April 10, 1898. Salt Lake City: The Church of Jesus Christ of Latter-Day Saints.

Smith, Joseph, translator. *The Book of Mormon, Another Testament of Christ*. Salt Lake City: The Church of Jesus Christ of Latter-day Saints, 1996.

_____, *Doctrine and Covenants*. Salt Lake City: The Church of Jesus Christ of Latter Day-Saints, 1996.

_____, *Pearl of Great Price*. Salt Lake City: The Church of Jesus Christ of Latter-Day Saints, 1996.

Widtsoe, John A. *Joseph Smith, Seeker After Truth, Prophet of God*. Salt Lake City: Deseret News Press, 1951.

Author's Note:

I find it extremely interesting that the late Fawn Brodie, the talented but literarily unethical apostate Mormon author who wrote a scurrilous biography of the Prophet Joseph Smith, for which she was excommunicated, should later decide to write a scurrilous biography of Thomas Jefferson also. Was this a mere coincidence of choice? Alf J. Mapp, Jr., in his excellent book listed above, effectively debunks the spurious nonsense included in Brodie's book.

Index

About the Author

John Stewart has been a university professor, LDS bishop, mayor, newspaperman, editor, author, rancher, freelance writer of syndicated columns and magazine articles.

A conservationist, he is president of the *Wellsville Mountain Corporation*. He was chief founder of the *Genealogy Club of America* and of the *National Association for Outlaw & Lawman History*.

He is president of the *Golden Spike Heritage Foundation* and vice president of the *Golden Spike Association*. Each May 10 he serves as master of ceremonies at the Golden Spike program at Promontory, Utah, commemorating completion of America's first transcontinental railroad.

The Stewarts live in Cache Valley, Utah and Teton Valley, Idaho.